Thomas Wardle

Monographs on the Tusser and other Wild Silks of India

descriptive of the objects and specimens exhibited in the India section of

the Paris Exhibition: and on the dyestuffs and tannin matters of India and

their native uses, descriptive of the collec

Thomas Wardle

Monographs on the Tusser and other Wild Silks of India
descriptive of the objects and specimens exhibited in the India section of the Paris Exhibition: and on the dyestuffs and tannin matters of India and their native uses, descriptive of the collec

ISBN/EAN: 9783337311162

Printed in Europe, USA, Canada, Australia, Japan

Cover: Foto ©Andreas Hilbeck / pixelio.de

More available books at **www.hansebooks.com**

PARIS UNIVERSAL EXHIBITION, 1878.

MONOGRAPHS

ON THE

Tusser and other Wild Silks of India, descriptive
of the Objects and Specimens exhibited in the
India Section of the Paris Exhibition,

AND ON THE

Dyestuffs and Tannin Matters of India and their
Native Uses, descriptive of the Collection in
the India Section of the Paris Exhibition ;

BY

THOMAS WARDLE, F.C.S., F.G.S.,

MEMBER OF JURY, CLASS 34.

LONDON:
PRINTED BY GEORGE E. EYRE AND WILLIAM SPOTTISWOODE,
PRINTERS TO THE QUEEN'S MOST EXCELLENT MAJESTY.
FOR HER MAJESTY'S STATIONERY OFFICE.
1878.

Price Fivepence.

Monograph on the Wild Silk Industry of India, illustrated by the Contents of the large Glass Case containing Wild Silk Specimens in the India Section.

It is the silk produced by the Tasar, Tusser or Tussore worm, in which the chief interest of the case lies.

I have endeavoured to exhibit this silk in as full a manner as the space assigned to me would permit, representing it in all states of its manufacture and tinctorial enrichment, showing the recent improvement in manufacture and dyeing of which it is capable, as well as illustrating the Natural History of the Tusser insect in all stages of its development, by preserved specimens of its several phases, except the larvæ, which it has not been possible to obtain.

Tusser silk has long been known and used by the natives of India. They have exported it in considerable quantities of late years, but from their imperfect mode of manipulating it in its earlier stages of manufacture, and from the difficulty of dyeing it well, it has made but little way in Europe except for ladies' and children's dresses in an undyed state.

In Bengal and the adjoining provinces from time immemorial the natives have manufactured this silk into cloth called "Tussehdoot'hies," which is worn by Brahmins and other sects of Hindoos.

In 1858 Dr. Birdwood brought the wild worms under the notice of this country, and urged their utilization.

The silk is found from the North-west range of the Himalaya south as far as Midnapore, in Bengal, and through the North-east range to Assam, and southward to Chittagong, and probably further. It is found also in the Presidencies of Bombay and Madras. It is said to be abundant in Bhagulpore in Bengal. It abounds chiefly in the Eastern districts of Chattisgarh, namely, Raipur, Bilaspur, and Sambulpur, in the Chanda district of the Nagpore province, and the Leone district.

The natural colour of the silk is a darkish shade of fawn, much unlike the golden and white colours of the Mulberry-worm silks.

It has much less affinity for dyestuffs, especially for those which grow in India, and it has not until recently been much dyed.

For several years I have been engaged with considerable success in improving the methods of dyeing, and the results are shown in the case, Nos. 10, 11, 12, 20, 40, 41, 42, 52.

Important improvements which I have had effected in the manufacture of Tusser silk are shown in Nos. 8, 9, 18, 19, 21, 51, 53, 54, 55, which will be fully described in their turn.

These improvements in the manufacture and dyeing are most likely to have a very great influence on the cultivation of this silk, and probably also of other wild silks, the demand for which may in a few years be only measured by the quantity which can be produced.

The first specimen under No. 1 in the case is a leaf of a species of Terminalia containing eggs of the Tusser moth, which are said to hatch in from two to four weeks.

The larvæ, when fully grown, are about four inches in length ; they have twelve joints or articulations, besides their extremities ; their colour is green resembling the leaves on which they feed ; and they are marked with reddish spots and a reddish yellow band running lengthways. They feed on several plants :—

> Rhizophora calceolaris. Linn.
> Terminalia alata glabra (Assum tree).
> Terminalia tomentosa (the Saj tree).
> Terminalia Catappa (Country Almond tree
> Tectona grandis. (Teak tree.)
> Zizyphus jujuba. (Ber tree.)
> Shorea robusta. (Sal tree.)
> Bombax heptaphyllum. (Semul.)
> Careya sphærica.
> Pentaptera tomentosa.
> Pentaptera glabra.
> Ricinus communis (Castor oil plant).
> Cassia lanceolata.

In six weeks from the time they are hatched they begin to spin their cocoons, which they most curiously suspend from the branches of the trees by constructing a thick hard cord or filament of silky matter, which is made to grasp the branches, as seen in the specimens No. 3.

As soon as the worm has spun its cocoon it takes the form of chrysalis or pupa (see No. 2), and remains a prisoner in the cocoons for about nine months, or from October until July. At the end of this time the chrysalis takes the form of a moth, and whilst its wings are in an imperfectly developed state it softens one end of the cocoons with an exudation which enables it to separate the filaments of silk and to work its way out of the cocoon. This it effects during the night.

Those shown under No. 4 are cocoons from which the moth has emerged.

No. 5.

Tusser cocoons from Sambulpur, in the Central Provinces, but larger than those under No. 3.

The weight of the ordinary Tusser cocoon with its pupa enclosed and the cord by which it is attached to the branch is about five grammes.

Nos. 6 and 7.

Are specimens of Tusser moths known under the following names :—

> Antherea Paphia (Linnæus).
> Bombyx „ (Hübner).
> Saturnia „ (Helfer).
> Phalæna Attacus Mylitta (Durmy).
> „ Paphia (Roxburgh).
> Bombyx Mylitta (Fabricius).
> "Bughy" of the native of Burbhoon Hills where the silk (which the same people call "Tussch") is manufactured.

The male is of a reddish pale brown colour and the female much yellower.

Mr. O'Neil in his report says :—" The moths are particularly " revered by the people engaged in the culture of the worms, the " occulili on their wing being considered as the 'chakra' or mark " of Vishnu. These people also pretend to observe the greatest " purity of life during the time they are in the jungles rearing " the worms, and also do not eat flesh, fish, or spices, do not shave " or cut their hair, do not wear washed clothing, nor anoint their " bodies with oil, and do not touch any of whom a relative may " have recently died."

Nos. 8 and 9.

Organzine and Tram Tusser of the quality and state of manufacture now used in England for weaving, and a good representation of the present state of its manufacture which gives a size of 255 deniers (15 drams per 1,000 yards). The sizes of the Tusser silk generally used in England run from 152 deniers (9 drams) to 255 deniers (15 drams). These are very coarse sizes and must necessarily be unfit to produce such fine textile work as the mulberry silk which is manufactured into Organzine and Tram of 21 deniers and upwards ($1\frac{1}{4}$ drams) and from which are made the finest silk fabrics.

The printed cloths Nos. 21 and 55 are made with Tusser Organzine and Tram of the coarse size of Nos. 8 and 9 and of the same quality.

The want of fineness and quality is owing to the imperfect and unskilful mode of manipulating it from the cocoon upwards in India, and the want of better machinery to prepare it in the raw state,

Nos. 10, 11, and 12.

The same silks dyed in colours and black. Nos. 10 and 12 are dyed entirely with Indian dyestuffs, and are well worthy of notice.

No. 13.

Native reeled Tusser raw silk, undyed. From Bhagulpur.

No. 14.

Another specimen of native-reeled Tusser raw silk, undyed.

No. 15.

The same silk dyed by the natives.

No. 16.

Native reeled Tusser raw silk, undyed. From Bogra.

No. 17.

Native reeled Tusser, from Bengal, undyed.

Leaving the question as to whether it can be successfully wound or not, one important consideration respecting its use presents itself, namely, its capability of being spun like cotton and wool. The great improvements made in late years in England in spinning machinery have proved that marvellous results in making an even thread from waste silk and unwindable cocoons for sewing and weaving purposes may be attained, and I will venture to predict a future for this and the produce of all unwindable silk worm cocoons that will compensate for their collection.

The industry of the natives should be stimulated to the gathering in of all kinds of wild silk cocoons, whether windable or not, for there is no doubt that those kinds which cannot be wound can be most easily spun, and there is at the present moment a request on the part of silk spinners for a larger supply of Tusser silk cocoons and Tussore silk waste, for spinning purposes, and no doubt other silk cocoons would be gladly bought up.

No. 25.

A sample of Eria silk, spun, no doubt by hand, by the natives.

No. 26.

The same imperfectly dyed by them.

No. 27.

Eria silk made by the Ricini-fed worm of Assam.

No. 28.

The same from another district of Assam (Lakhimpur).

Nos. 29 & 30.

Are specimens, male and female, of the moth :—

Attacus Atlas (Hübner).
Phalæna Attacus Atlas (Linnæus).
Bombyx Atlas (Fabricius).

This moth feeds on the Phyllanthus emblica.

No. 30.

Is a specimen of the cocoon of this splendid moth which might easily be spun.

No. 31.

Actias Selene ;
Phalæna Attacus ;

Feeds on Munsooree (Coriaria nipalensis). The cocoon is enclosed between two leaves. The silk does not appear to be windable, but is of a coarsish kind and might also be spun.

No. 32.

Cocoons of Actias Selene.

Nos. 33 & 34.

Moths, male and female, and cocoons of Bombyx Attacus (Yam Mai).

Although this insect is a native of Japan it is found also in China and India.

In Japan the silk of this worm is said to be most highly prized and reserved for the use of Royalty, but this I am inclined to doubt, as the silk is not fine, the cocoon is of a beautiful pale green colour.

It has been naturalized in Europe.

A cross between the Yama Mai and Bombyx Attacus Pernyi is a great success in France. It is so hardy that hatching is said to take place at freezing point.

Nos. 35 & 36.

Cocoons and silk of the Mooga or Moonga worm, Antherea Assama.

There are five breeds of this worm per year. The feed on the Addakoory, Champa, Soona, Kontooloa, Digluttee, Pattee, Shoonda, and Souhalloo.

Promises to be a useful silk under proper care.

No. 37.

A silk catled Ya-baine from the district of Prome, Burmah, the produce of the Bombyx Mori.

No. 38.

Eggs, cocoons, moss, and silk grège of the Bombyx Mori. This is the Bengal silk of commerce. The worms feed on the leaves of the Mulberry tree as in China, Japan, and Europe.

No. 39.

" Pat " silk. A rare kind of silk from Assam, probably a variety of Bombyx Mori, but stated to be the produce of Bombyx Texta. The worm is fed on the Mulberry leaf.

No. 40.

A rare silk from Mezankuri, Assam.

No. 41.

Another specimen of " Pat " or " Pat Suta " silk with cocoons. A mulberry silk from Assam.

Nos. 42 & 43.

A set of Tusser patterns dyed with Aniline colours.

These are placed here to show the shades Aniline dyes can be made to give on this silk, and not as a recommendation of their use in this direction. The native dyestuffs will give more permanent colours, properly mordanted. Aniline dyes are fugitive, and their use for artistic purposes or for goods intended to last a long time cannot be too seriously lamented.

No. 44.

This is a sample of ordinary Bengal Organzine, dyed with a dye-stuff common in most parts of British India, not used, as far as I know, in Europe.

It is the powder brushed off the capsules of the Mallotus Phil-lipensis, called in India "Kapila" or "Kamala," which contains 70 to 80 per cent. of colouring matter. By mordanting the silk with carbonate of soda and alum, the powder yields a rich variety of shades of golden yellow and orange colours. It appears to be worthy of the notice of European dyers.

Nos. 45 and 51.

A series of patterns to show to what uses the waste of Tusser silk and the cocoons pierced by the exit of the moth can be put by spinning in the same way threads of cotton and wool are manu-factured. It commences with samples of pierced cocoons which could not be wound, waste silk from ordinary Tusser manufacture, and followed by samples showing the various processes the silk undergoes before it is made into thread or cord for weaving or for sewing purposes.

This suggests forcibly a promising economy in store for the pro-duce of all silk-making worms. There are many species unknown to commerce, rejected because of their not being capable of being wound in the ordinary way, but, as I have before stated, now spinning machinery is in such a perfect state, all cocoons may be spun and converted into materials of some use or other. In Simla alone, there are said to be eight or nine species of Bombyx, which no doubt might be utilized in this way.

These remarks lead me to describe—

Nos. 53 and 54,

which are patterns of spun Tusser made in the way and from the material I have just described, threads of various sizes for sewing and weaving purposes as well as for fringes and knitting, dyed and undyed. They may be dyed almost any shade.

No. 56.

Are fabrics made of this spun Tusser, woven undyed, in several designs for me by Messrs. Clayton, Marsdens, Holden, & Co., silk spinners, of Halifax, who also made me the samples 45 to 57 from pierced cocoons and waste Tussore with which I furnished them, from material collected for me in India by order of the Govern-ment of India.

No. 57.

A pattern of the same kind as No. 56, but which I have printed in seven colours.

No. 57a.

Cocoons of the Bengal Mulberry silk, Bombyx Mori.

No. 58.

Grége, or raw fine Bengal silk from Ragshaye district.

No. 59.

A skein of Bengal yellow raw silk from Ragshaye district.

No. 60.

A skein of Bengal White raw silk from Ragshaye district.

No. 61.

Cocoons of " Poh " silk (Attacus Ricini) from Fonghoo, Burmah.

No. 62.

" Poh " raw silk (Attacus Ricini) Fonghoo, Burmah.

No. 63.

Cocoons of Moonga or Muga silk (Antherœa Assama), Ramrup, Assam.

No. 64.

Grége Moonga or Muga silk from Ramrup, Assam.

No. 65.

Cocoons and spun silk, not exported ; 100 maunds made annually.

No. 66.

Cocoons and raw silk " Pat " from Ramrup, Assam.   Bombyx texta.

No. 67.

Cocoons of Tusser silk from Beerbhoom, Bengal.

No. 68.

Black and drab cloth made from Tusser silk.   Price in December 1877 Rs. 6 a than, or R. 1 per yard.   From Sambulpur, Central Provinces.

No. 69.

Plain Tusser silk cloth.   Price in December 1877 Rs. 5 per piece.   From Sambulpur, Central Provinces.

No. 70.

Tusser silk cloth.   District Belaspur.   Central Provinces.

No. 71.

Interesting piece of dyed Tusser cloth, maroon plaid.

No. 72.

Piece of Tusser cloth, black and natural colour.

No. 73.

Piece of Tusser cloth, natural colour with stripe.

These cloths have all the defect of being too highly sized. They would be more marketable in Europe without the sizing, and feel and look much better.

Tusser silk is, therefore, proved to be capable of extended use, both from the improved manufacture I have spoken of, and from the circumstances that it is capable of being dyed and printed in the greatest variety of colours, and that the refuse portions can be spun into threads for such a variety of purposes that there need be no waste ; and I am thankful to have had the honour of being entrusted to point out the extended usefulness and application of the Tusser, and all other species of wild silks.

I attach a tabular statement of microscopic measurements of the primary fibre of Tusser and other silks, which I have made for the purpose of comparison.

                    (Signed)   THOS. WARDLE,
June 18th, 1878.   Leek, Staffordshire.

MICROSCOPIC MEASUREMENTS of the DIAMETER of the PRIMARY FIBRE of TUSSORE SILK and of other SILKS.

Names of Worms or Moths producing Silks.		Country.	Food of Larvae.	Measurement of the Diameter of the Primary Fibre.			
				French Metric Scale.		English Scale.	
Scientific Names.	Vernacular Names.			Loose Silk on Outside of Cocoons.	Silk forming Substance of Cocoons.	Loose Silk on Outside of Cocoons.	Silk forming Substance of Cocoons.
Bombyx mori	—	China	Mulberry	—	·0125 mm.	—	$\frac{1}{5800}$ in.
„ „ (white)	—	Japan	„	—	·0135 „	—	$\frac{1}{1500}$ „
„ „ (yellow)	—	Bengal	„	—	·006 „	—	$\frac{1}{3750}$ „
„ Ya-baine		Prome (Burmah)	„	—	·0083 „	—	$\frac{1}{3070}$ „
„ Brutia		Brutia, Asia Minor	„	—	·01 „	—	$\frac{1}{2750}$ „
„		Italian	„	—	·0115 „	—	$\frac{1}{2150}$ „
„		French	„	—	·0108 „	—	$\frac{1}{2300}$ „
„ texta	"Pat" Silk, bari palu	Assam	„	—	·0135 „	—	$\frac{1}{1733}$ „
Attacus ricini	Eria, Ailanthus	India	Ricinus Communis, or Castor-oil plant.	·016 mm.	·01 „	$\frac{1}{1800}$ in.	$\frac{1}{2350}$ „
Antheræa Assama	Mugah or Moongah	Assam	Soom and Sonhaloo trees.	·0135 „	·006 „	$\frac{1}{1858}$ „	$\frac{1}{2500}$ „
Antheræa Paphia (Tussore)	Nistari Polu koa "Tasar," "Tusser"	Beerbhoom(Bengal) India	Terminalia and other plants.	·01 „ None	·006 „ ·03125 „	$\frac{1}{2500}$ „ None	$\frac{1}{3750}$ „ $\frac{1}{800}$ „
Bombyx	Mezankuri Silk (rare)	Sibsagar (Assam) India	Mulberry	—	·01 „	—	$\frac{1}{2500}$ „
Actias selene	—	Mussooree, India	Coriaria nepalensis	·03 mm.	·02 „	$\frac{1}{730}$ in.	$\frac{1}{1250}$ „
Attacus Atlas	—	—	Phylanthus emblica, etc.	·03 „	·02 „	$\frac{1}{830}$ „	$\frac{1}{1750}$ „
Bombyx Attacus (the Oak Silk-worm).	Yama mai	India	The Oak	·025 „	·026 „	$\frac{1}{1000}$ „	$\frac{1}{830}$ „
Bombyx Attacus pernyi	—	China	„	—	·025 „	—	$\frac{1}{1000}$ „

MONOGRAPH ON THE DYESTUFFS AND TANNIN MATTERS
OF INDIA, EXPLANATORY OF THE SPECIMENS EXHIBITED
IN THE INDIA SECTION, BY THOMAS WARDLE.

Nos. 1 and 1a. ACACIA ARABICA.

This tree is very common in India, growing in all parts of
Bengal, Coromandel and the Deccan.

Vernacular
- (Bengalese, Hindustani, Mah-
ratti) - - - - Babul.
- (Burmese) - - - - Nan-lung Kyen.
- (Tamil) - - - - Karivelam.

The bark may be turned to advantage by the dyer in many
ways, and is also much used in India for tanning leather. By
simply boiling it in water it is made to produce various shades of
brown, and by adding during boiling catechu, the produce of the
plant treated of under Nos. 3 and 4 (Acacia catechu), and lime, a
somewhat permanent dye is obtained. By adding, instead of
catechu and lime, sulphate of iron, a black dye is produced. In
Sindh this bark is the chief produce of lac; and in Midnapur,
where it is termed "Babla," it is made to dye a very good drab
on cotton fabrics. Soap also is obtained from it.

As well as the bark the leaves and pods have in India various
tinctorial uses as yet unknown in the dyeing industry of Europe.

Nos. 2 and 3. ACACIA CATECHU.

Vernacular
- (Burm.) - Shea-dza.
- (Hind.) - Katha.
- (Tamil) - Kash katti.

This is one of the most common trees on the Bombay coast and
its Ghaut jungles, it is also found on the Malabar and Coromandel
coasts, the Northern Circars, and in the Dekhan; it grows, too, at
Serampore, Delhi, Nepaul, and other parts of India.

An extract of the wood is the catechu of commerce which has
been used for a long time in Europe very extensively for dyeing
browns on silks.

No. 4. ÆGLE MARMELOS.

Vernacular
- (Beng.) - Bel.
- (Burm.) - Oo-sheet.
- (Tel.) - Maradu chettu.

This is a common plant in waste places, inland forests, and old
gardens on the Bombay side of India. It is known in England
as "Bengal quince."

The part of the plant which is useful tinctorially is the pulp of
the fruit which produces a yellow dye. This pulp is also astringent.

No. 5. Aqynica Cecinia.

A tree found in Pegu, and known in the Burmese language by the following names :—

H'ta h'men.
Il'soke gyee.

At present it appears to be unknown to European dyers, but the bark, pounded, mixed with water, and sifted is used in India by fishermen for dyeing their nets, to which it imparts a deep red colour, and, by virtue of a kind of gum which it contains, protects the nets from the bad effects of the water.

No. 6. Aloes Sp.

Vernacular -
- *(Burm.)* - Mok.
- *(Hind.)* - Alia.
  - Elva.
  - Musabbar.
- *(Tel.)* - Mussambram.

A dye is produced from various species of this genus of plants and known under the same name. It is prepared from a bitter resinous juice stored up in greenish vessels lying beneath the skin or epidermis of the leaf. The leaves are cut transversely, and the juice which exudes is gradually evaporated into a firm consistence, in which state it is seen in the specimen in the case and is known in commerce. By proper preparation with several other ingredients it is made to produce an almond colour.

No. 7. Alum.

Vernacular -
- *(Hind.)* - Phatakri.
  - Tawas.
- *(Tel.)* - Pathcaramu.

This substance, so well known and so largely used in Europe as a mordant, both in dyeing and printing on cloth, has not hitherto been produced to any very considerable extent in India. At Kalabag on the Indus, however, it is manufactured from a sort of slate which is found in vast quantities in the neighbouring mountains. There are at Kalabag 14 manufactories for the purification of this mineral, the effluvia from which, especially in the heat of summer, greatly add to the natural unwholesomeness of the atmosphere. These manufactories produce annually about 430 tons, which is sold at 78 rupees per ton. There are also alum works at Kutch and at Kotkee in the Punjab. Alum occurs native in Nepaul and at Chownsilla.

No. 8. Amaranthus Polygamus.

Vernacular -
- *(Beng.)* - Champa nuti.
- *(Hind.)* - Chumli sag.
  - Chulai.
- *(Tam.)* - Mulli kirey.

This plant is cultivated all over Southern Asia. Its ashes are mixed with Tarota seeds, lime, and indigo, for dyeing shades of colour varying from blue to black.

No. 9. AMYGDALUS PERSICA.

Vernacular -$\begin{cases} (Ars.) & \text{- Khookh.} \\ (Hind.) & \text{- Shaft-aloo.} \end{cases}$

A variety of the peach tree, apparently not yet known in European tinctorial industry. It grows in the vicinity of Shanghae.

No. 10. ANILIA SAK.

This is the Indian name for a dyeing material, of which the specimen marked No. 10 is a sample, but which is not known at present, as far as I can gather in Europe.

Nos. 11 and 12. ARTOCARPUS INTEGRIFOLIA.

Vernacular -$\begin{cases} (Hind.) & \text{- Pannas.} \\ (Beng.) & \text{- Kantal.} \\ (Burm.) & \text{- Peing-nai.} \\ (Mahr.) & \text{- Fanuas.} \\ (Tam.) & \text{- Pila maram.} \end{cases}$

This tree, known to Englishmen by the name of " Jack tree " or " Jack fruit tree," is indigenous to and grows freely in Pegu and Bassim. The wood is used for dyeing light to deep shades of golden yellow on silk and cotton. It is mainly used for dyeing the robes of the Burmese monks. If combined with " Iltouksha " or vitex arborea it gives a light green, which is permanent.

No. 15. BAHAKAR.

An Indian dyeing material not used at present, as far as I am aware, in Europe.

No. 16. BASSIA LATIFOLIA.

Vernacular -$\begin{cases} (Beng.) & \text{- Mohwa.} \\ (Hind.) & \text{- Mahwa.} \\ (Mahr.) & \text{- Moho.} \\ (Tam.) & \text{- Illupa.} \end{cases}$

A tree known in England as the Mahwa tree, growing in the mountainous parts of the Circars, in Bengal, the Terace, Oudh, Gwalior, Punjab, in Malwa, Nagpore, and Guzerat.
The bark is used in India along with other ingredients for dyeing a beautiful golden yellow on cotton.

No. 13. CURCUMA LONGA.

Turmeric powder of which No. 13 in the case is a sample, it will be found more fully described under No. 54.

No. 14. Bhushee.

This is another name for carbonate of soda, quod vide.

No. 17. Bauhinia Purpurea.

Vernacular { (*Beng.*) - Deva Kanchun.
(*Mahr.*) - Kunchun.
(*Tel.*) - Bodanta Chettu.

This tree which is a variety óf B. variegata and synonymous with B. acuminata and B. purpurascens grows throughout the year in the Mauritius, Ceylon, Assam, and both peninsulas of India. It is rare in Coimbatore and does not seem to be indigenous on the Bombay side where it is cultivated as also in the Punjab, the Dekhan, and Tenasserim.

At present it appears to be unknown tinctorially in Europe but has probably the same dyeing properties as B. variegata which is described under No. 18. In England it is known under the name of the "Purple mountain ebony."

No. 18. Bauhinia Variegata.

Vernacular { (*Beng.*) - Racto Kanchan.
(*Mahr.*) - Kanchan.
(*Hind.*) - Kuchnar.

A tree common in India, found in Burmah and at Ajmeer and sparingly in the Bombay forests. The bark is used in India as an ingredient in dyeing yellows on cotton.

The tree is known in England as the "mountain ebony," and it will be observed that its vernacular names somewhat resemble those of B. purpurea, which is a variety of it.

Nos. 19 and 20. Berberis Lycium.

Vernacular { (*Hind.*) { - Chitra.
- Kashmal.
- Sumulu.

Known in England as the Raisin Berberry, and found at an elevation of from 3,000 ft. to 9,000 ft. on the Himalaya, and at Missuri and Kaghan but not west of Hazara.

The root and wood yield a beautiful yellow dye.

Nos. 22 and 23. Berberis Tinctorium.

Vernacular { (the tree) (*Hind.*) - "Chitra" or "Chotra."
(the extract) (*Hind.*) - "Rusot" or "Rasaut."

This tree is well known in European tinctorial industry, and has in fact received the name of "Dyers' berberry." It ranges in the mountains of India from the Himalaya to the Neilgherries and to Newera Ellia in Ceylon.

Both root and wood contain a beautiful yellow colouring matter which exists in the root to the extent of $17°/_{o}$. This yellow colouring principle according to Leschenault is contained by B. tinctoria in a greater state of purity than by the common English Berberry. This tree is said to be identical with B. aristata.

No. 24. BHAURI LEAVES.

A dyeing material used in India for the preparation of a red colour and found in the jungles. The Mahratti name is Shunkrong-blai.

No. 25. BHUSHEE OR BHUSKI.

Identical with Carbonate of Soda, quod vide.

No. 26. BIXA ORELLANA.

Vernacular
- (*Beng. & Hind.*) - Latkan.
- (*Burm.*) - - Thiden.
- (*Mahr.*) - - Kisree.
- (*Tel.*) - - Jaffra Chettu.

Synonymous with Bixaceae orellacea.   There are two varieties of this plant, " Cariboea " with rose coloured flowers cultivated in the West Indies, and " Indica " with white flowers cultivated in India.   The pulp of the seed forms the arnotto of commerce so extensively used as a dye for silks and cloths of many descriptions. A great variety of very beautiful red and orange colours are obtained by it, and by mixing it with other dyes.   It is also much used as a colouring matter for cheese.   The dye of the Indian variety, however, is neither so good nor so abundant as that of the West Indies.   The plant is much cultivated in Singapore, Mysore, and the northern parts of India.   Dr. McClelland mentions that it is largely cultivated all over Pegu for the red and yellow dyeing properties of its capsule.

No. 27. BOKAL BARK.

Vernacular
- (*Beng., Hind., Sans.*) - Bakula.
- (*Burm.*) - - Kya-ya.
- (*Mahr.*) - - Bacul.
- (*Hind.*) - - Mulsari.

The bark of a tree botanically known as Mimusops elengi.   The tree is found in Ceylon, throughout the peninsulas and the north of India, in Burmah, Pegu, Tenasserim and the Moluccas.   In the Bombay forests it is mostly found as a cultivated tree, more rarely wild and then only below the Ghats.   The bark is used for dyeing various shades of drab on cotton.

No. 28. BUCHANIA LATIFOLIA (ROXB.).

Vernacular
- (*Burm.*) - Lumbo.
- (*Hind.*) - Pyal.
- (*Mahr.*) - Char.
- (*Sanse.*) - Chara.
- (*Tel.*) - Chara chettu.

A tree common for some distance west of Jumna in the lower hills.   It also grows in Ajmeer and in the Bombay presidency, where it is found in the inland districts more than the coast jungles. In Canara and Sunda it is most frequent among the Ghats particularly north of Dandellee.   It abounds, too, in Mysore and Cuddapah, and occurs in Cuttack.   The bark is used for tanning.

Nos. 29 and 30.   BUTEA FRONDOSA.   (ROXB.)

Vernacular -
- (*Beng.*) - Pulasa.
- (*Burm.*) - Pouk pin.
- (*Hind.*) - Parasa.
- (*Mahr.*) - Pullus.
- (*Sansc.*) - Kinouka.
- (*Tel.*) - Tella moduga.

This plant occurs in most parts of India.   An infusion of its flowers and also of those of B. superba produce on cotton, previously mordanted with alum, a great variety of beautiful yellow colours, and by the application of an alkali to the cotton subsequently to dyeing a deep reddish orange can be obtained.   The seeds are also useful to the dyer, producing on cotton a light yellowish salmon colour.   During the last five years, in Nagpur, the crops of Butea flowers have, altogether, amounted to 500,000 maunds.   In Oudh the price is 2s. to 16s. per kutcha maund. This plant in England is called the Pulas tree.

No. 31.   CAESALPINIA CORIARIA (WILLD.).

A plant found in gardens in Madras, growing plentifully also about Singapore, Salem, Bangalore, Hoonsoor, and Chicacole.   It was introduced into India in 1842 by Dr. Wallich.   The seed pods are extensively used for dyeing several varieties of black and for tanning leather.   The selling price of the pods with the seeds removed is from 8l. to 13l. per ton.   They are known in English by the names of " Libi libi," " Divi divi," and American sumach.

No. 32.   CAESALPINIA SAPPAN (LINN.).

Vernacular -
- (*Beng.*) - Bakkam.
- (*Hind.*) - Pattangay.
- (*Mahr.*) - Pattang.

This tree grows all over S.E. Asia.   Its wood, 3,000 or 4,000 tons of which are annually imported into Ehgland, is used for dyeing reds on silk.

No. 33.   CALOTROPIS GIGANTEA (BROWN).

Vernacular -
- (*Burm.*) - Mai-oh.
- *Hind.*) - { Akund. / Ak.
- (*Tel.*) - Tella jilledu.

A tree growing all over India and Burmah, the fibre from which is used for making a cloth which is said to be very durable. The bark, termed Madar bark, is said to have tinctorial properties.

No. 34.   CALYSACCION LONGIFOLIUM (ROXB.)

Vernacular -
- (*Burm.*) - Tha-ra-bi.
- (*Can.*) - Taringa.
- (*Tel.*) - Sura ponna.
- Surunji (in Ahmednagar).

A tree growing on the Northern Circars, Konkans, Kennari Jungles, and Western Mysore.   The roots and bark are used in

Ahmednagar along with the flowers of Grislea tomentosa and the fruit of Terminalia chebula for dyeing cloth a green colour. The flower buds are also said to have tinctorial properties upon silk.

No. 35. CARTHAMUS TINCTORIA.

Vernacular -
(*Hind.*)	-	Kusum.
(*Sansc.*)	-	Kusumbha.
(*Tam.*)	-	Sendurgan.
(*Tel.*)	-	Agnisikha.

This plant is grown in great abundance all over India, and the flowers, which have received the name of Safflower, are largely exported, and also used by the native dyers. The safflower from Paterghanta and Belispore is considered in the London market to be the best exported from India. With regard to the inland trade the quantity exported to the town of Nagar alone during the year 1874–5 was valued at about Rs. 12,000, about two-thirds of which were sent to Bombay, and the rest consumed locally. Safflower is exported in large quantities from the Nizam's dominions, and commands a price of Rs. 20 to Rs. 40 per palla of 120 seers, while that produced in the district of Ahmednagar sells at Rs. 15 per palla. It is used for dyeing silk and cotton to which it imparts beautiful shades of pink and scarlet.

No. 36. CASSIA AURICULATA.

Vernacular -
(*Hind.*)	-	Tarwar.
(*Tel.*)	-	Tangada Kurra.

The bark of this tree, which grows in Madras and the Deccan, is useful for tanning leather. The value of the quantity produced in the district of Ahmednagar annually is Rs. 25,000, of which four-fifths are sent to the Bombay markets and one-fifth consumed locally.

No. 37. CASSIA FISTULA.

Vernacular -
(*Tam.*)	-	Koannay.
(*Mal.*)	-	Choonnay.
(*Tel.*)	-	Kela.
(*Hind.*)	-	Amultas.
(*Beng.*)	-	Sonaloo.

Synonymous with Carthartocarpus fistula. The bark of this tree is used for tanning, but not being very astringent is of no great value. In England this tree is known as the "Pudding Pipe tree."

No. 38. CASSIA TORA.

Vernacular -
(*Beng. & Hind.*)	-	Chakunda.
(*Sansc.*)	- -	Prabunatha.
(*Tam.*)	- -	Tagary.

The seeds of this plant called Tartigyan seeds are used in the preparation of a blue dye which is fixed by lime water. The plant abounds all over the plains of India and in Tenasserim.

No. 39. CASUARINA MURICATA.

Vernacular -
$\begin{cases} (Burm.) & - & \text{H'ten-roo.} \\ (Hind.) & - & \text{Hari.} \end{cases}$

A tree grown in all paris of the Deccan, where it was introduced in 1830, and diffused over Bengal. A brown dye has been extracted from its bark. Its wood is known in England as " Beefwood."

No. 40. CARTHARTOCARPUS FISTULA.

Synonymous with Cassia fistula quod vide.

No. 41. CEDRELA TOONA (ROXB.).

Vernacular -
$\begin{cases} (Beng., Sansc.) & - & \text{Tunna.} \\ (in~Bombay) & - & \text{Kooruk.} \\ (Burm.) - & - & \text{Thit-ka-do.} \\ (Hind.) - & - & \text{Toona.} \\ (Tam.) - & - & \text{Toona maram.} \end{cases}$

The tree grows at the foot of the Himalaya and to the south, in Bengal, Mysore, and both peninsulas of India in varying abundance. It is said to exist plentifully in Travancore. Its flowers are useful in dyeing nankeens on cotton, and will produce a good fawn colour on unbleached calico. In conjunction with safflower they are used by the natives of Mysore for dyeing the beautiful red colour there known as " Gul-i-Nari." The bark is very astringent. The tree is known in England under the name of Toon tree.

No. 42. CERCOPS ROXBURGHIANUS.

Vernacular -
$\begin{cases} (Beng.) & - & \text{Garan.} \\ (Burm.) & - \begin{cases} \text{Ka-by-ain.} \\ \text{Kn-byen.} \end{cases} \end{cases}$

A tree growing on all the coasts of tropical Asia. The bark is used among dyers in India, chiefly in the presidency of Bengal.

No. 43. CHAIKATHA.

A tree growing in the Balasore district, an infusion of the wood and roots of which produces a light drab colour on cotton.

No. 44. CITRUS ACIDA.

Vernacular - (Hind.) - Limbu-ka-chal.

The lemon tree, the rind of the fruit of which, in Shikarpur, is used in dyeing as a mordant.

No. 45. COCCUS CACTI.

Vernacular -
$\begin{cases} (Guz., Hind., Pers. & - & \text{Kermij.} \\ (Tam.) & - & \text{Cochinil puchi.} \\ (Tel.) & - & \text{Cochinil puruga.} \end{cases}$

An insect, a native of Mexico, the dried bodies of which constitute the substance known as cochineal, which is so extensively used as a dye, and which imparts to silk and wool such splendid and permanent shades of red, crimson, and scarlet. Great Britain pays annually about 440,000*l.* for this insect (1870), considerably more than 1,000 tons being imported every year, and purchased at about 3*s.* 6*d.* per lb. Cochineal is an expensive colour, and is rarely in the hands of the Indian native dyer, but if supplied to him he understands the method of using it. The Coccus cacti is, at seasons, plentiful in many parts of India, and Sir Charles Layard informs me, also in Ceylon. It was introduced into India in the year 1799. The insects feed upon the prickly pear (Cactus indicus) and swarm to localities where it grows ; 70,000 of them weigh only 1 lb. The use of cochineal has most unfortunately been immensely restricted since the discovery of the reds derived from aniline, to the great detriment of lasting dyes, as cochineal when used with proper mordants is very permanent and gives a great variety of shades.

No. 46. Coccus Lacca.

Vernacular - { (*In Nagpur*) - Lakh.
{ (*In Mergui*) - Khyril.
{ Lakh Dana.

The insect which produce the substance called lac. It inhabits India and is found on various trees in great abundance on Ficus religiosa, F. Indica, Butea frondosa, and Rhamnus jujuba. When the females of this coccus have fixed themselves to a part of the branch of the tree on which they feed, a pellucid and glutinous substance begins to exude from the margins of the body, and in the end this substance covers the whole insect with a cell which when hardened by exposure to the air becomes lac. So numerous are these insects, and so closely crowded together that they often entirely cover a branch. The broken twigs covered with these incrustations are called stick lac. After the colour has been extracted and further purified shellac results. Lac is used as a bright red dye on wool and other cloths and for some purposes instead of cochineal. It is largely manufactured in Bengal.

No. 47. Conocarpus Latifolius (Roxb.)

Vernacular - { (*Hind.*) - Thoura.
{ (*Mahr.*) - Dawura.
{ (*Tel.*) - Duca.

This tree grows in the Kenneri jungles, valleys of the Konkan rivers, on the inland Dekhan hills, and at Chillaime and Chittagong. The leaves are used for dyeing yellow, and the gum from the tree for a thickening for the colouring liquid in printing on cloth.

No. 48. Copper.

Vernacular - { (*Burm.*) - Ky-a-ni.
{ (*Mal.*) - Tambaga.
{ (*Sansc.*) - Tamraka.
{ (*Tam.*) - Shembu.
{ (*Tel.*) - Tambram.

Copper ores occur in the Jepoor dominions, in the vicinity of Nagpore, in the form of sulphuret chiefly in Ramgurh, and the carbonate in Ajmeer.

No. 49. COPPERAS.

Vernacular -
- (*Hind.*) - Mortuth.
- (*Sansc.*) - Tulthanjana.
- (*Tam.*) - Turishu.
- (*Tel.*) - Turishi.

This substance is largely manufactured in several parts of India.

No. 50. COSCINIUM FENESTRATUM.

Vernacular -
- (*Tam.*) - Mara munjib.
- (*Tel.*) - Mani pasupu.

A tree which grows in Ceylon and Southern India. Its wood yields a yellow dye.

No. 51. CROTALARIA JUNCEA.

Vernacular -
- (*Hind.*) - Sunn.
- (*Burm.*) - Pan.
- (*Tam.*) - Wakkoo.
- (*Tel.*) - Sannamu.

This plant is cultivated for its fibre in many parts of India.

No. 52. CURCUMA AMADA.

Vernacular -
- (*Beng.*) - Amada.
- (*Malay.*) - Tommon Munga.

A plant of Guzerat, Concan, and Bengal.

No. 53. CURCUMA AROMATICA.

Synonymous with C. Zedoaria quod vide.

Nos. 54, 55, 56, 57, 58. CURCUMA LONGA (ROXB.)

Vernacular -
- (*Beng., Hind.*) - Haldi.
- (*Malay.*) - Hoonhet.
- (*Sansc.*) - Haridra.
- (*Tam.*) - Munjall.
- (*Tel.*) - Pasupu.

A plant which grows all over India and the Archipelago. The root is known as turmeric and is a dyestuff which is very extensively used. It imparts very bright yellows to silks and when used along with indigo green colours are obtained. On Tussah silk turmeric produces a gold colour. It is very fugitive but in several parts of the east the colour is successfully fixed by mordanting.

No. 58a. CURCUMA TURMERICA.

No. 59. Curcuma Zedoaria.

Vernacular - { *(Beng.)* - - Shuthif.
(Hind., Sansc., Tel.) - Kuchur, Karchura.)
(Tam.) - - Kasturi manjab.

A plant indigenous to Bengal, Chittagong, and China. In England it has the name of the "long-leaved turmeric," and like C. Longa yields a yellow dye.
This is an interesting collection of the species of Curcuma although not complete. I believe all of them yield a yellow dye. They are also severally used in perfumery, medicine, and as a condiment.

No. 60. Datisca Camialbina.

Vernacular - *(Hind.)* - Ik'l-bir.

A tree growing in Cashmere, Kanawur, Nepal, and the Himalaya. The bark and root are esteemed in the Punjab for dyeing yellow.

No. 61. Delphinium Pp.

Vernacular - *(in Ahmednagar)* - Espharka palli.

This species of Delphinium is used in Ahmednagar along with pistachio galls for dying light red.

No. 62. Diospyros Sp.

Vernacular - Dhanbaher.

A tree of India, the bark of which is used for tanning leather.

No. 63. Diospyros Haspi. (The Ebony Tree.)

Vernacular - *(Kendu.)* - Tai.

A tree growing in Henzada, by which is yielded a dyeing material which is exhibited in a liquid state in the case.

No. 64. Carbonate of Soda.

Vernacular - { *(Guz., Hind.)* - Sajikhar.
(Hind.) - Khar.
(Tam., Tel.) - Applacaram.

In India carbonate of soda is obtained from Salicornia Arabica. West of Surdurbuns, and from Salicornia Indica, west of Malabar. It is extensively used for washing and cleaning fabrics and textile materials of every description previously to dyeing.

No. 65. Emblica Officinalis.

Vernacular - { *(Beng.)* - Aoula.
(Malay) - Malaca.
(Hind.) - Amliki.
(Tam.) - Nellikai.
(Tel.) - Amla kanni.

A tree growing in south of Peninsula and the Southern Mahratta country. The fruit produces a very good slate colour on cotton and the bark is used for tanning leather.

No. 66. EMBRYOPTERIS GLUTINIFERA.

Vernacular -
{ (*Beng., Hind.*) - Gal.
{ (*Tam.*) - - Tumbika.
{ (*Tel.*) - - Tumei.

This plant grows in the north of Ceylon, the Peninsula, Travancore, and Bengal. An infusion of the unripe fruit, which
contains a very large proportion of tannin, is used for steeping
fishing nets to make them more durable.

No. 67. EUGENIA JAMBOLANA.

Vernacular -
{ (*Beng.*) - Kalo jam.
{ (*Hind.*) - Burra jamon.
{ (*Mahr.*) - Jambool.
{ (*Tam.*) - Peru nagal.
{ (*Tel.*) - Pedda neredu.

A plant growing in Madras, Bombay, and other parts of India.
It is used with indigo in dyeing cotton yarns blue.

No. 68. EUPHORBIA TIRUCALLI.

Vernacular -
{ (*Beng.*) - Lauka sij.
{ (*Hind.*) - Sendh.
{ (*Mahr.*) - Seyr teg.
{ (*Tel.*) - Jemudu.

The plant grows on the Bombay side, in Coromandel, Malabar,
and Bengal. It is known in England as the "Milk hedge."

No. 69. FICUS INFECTORIA.

Vernacular -
{ (*Can.*) - Bassari mara.
{ (*Hind.*) - Jovi.
{ (*Tel.*) - Juvvi.

A plant growing in Ceylon and the peninsula of India. The
root furnishes a red dye for cloth.

No. 70. FICUS RELIGIOSA.

Vernacular -
{ (*Beng.*) - Ashwuth.
{ (*Hind.*) - Pipal.
{ (*Tam.*) - Arasa maram.
{ (*Tel.*) - Raya manu.

This tree grows in most of the countries of S.E. Asia. In Midnapur the bark, which is termed "Asud chal," is used to produce
a reddish drab on cotton. The leaves are used for tanning
leather.

No. 71. FULLER'S EARTH.

Vernacular - (*in Shikarpur*) - Mait.

Of this substance 4,000 maunds annually are produced at Rohri
and sent to Shikarpur, where it is bought at Rs. 5 per maund. It
is used for cleaning silk and wool previously to dyeing.

No. 72.   Garcinia Roxburghia.

Vernacular - $\begin{cases} (Burm.) & - & \text{Toung-tha-lay.} \\ (Hind.) & - & \text{Cowa.} \end{cases}$

This tree grows in Ceylon, Travancore, Malabar, Chittagong, and on the hills of British Burmah. A light yellow dye is extracted from the bark.

No. 73.   Gul Jullil.

Silk is steeped into a solution of this substance, which is found in Hyderabad, previously to being dyed yellow with turmeric. I do not know the botanical name, but the dye is obtained from the pale yellow flowers and stalks.

No. 74.   Gossypium Indicum.

Vernacular - $\begin{cases} (Beng.) & \cdots \begin{cases} \text{Kapase.} \\ \text{Tula.} \end{cases} \\ (Burm.) & - & \text{Wa.} \\ (Hind.) & - & \text{Kapas.} \end{cases}$

The cotton plant, which grows in Hyderabad, Jacobabad, and other parts of India. The flowers, called in Jacobabad " Vonum-jo-gul," are used as a mordant in dyeing various colours.

No. 75.   Grewia Oppositifolia.

Vernacular - $\begin{cases} (Hind.) & - & \text{Daman.} \\ (Sindi, Panj.) & - & \text{Bihull.} \end{cases}$

A plant which grows in the Kheree Pass and in the Dheera Dhoon, and is found in the Sutlej Valley, between Rangpur and Sungnam. I am not yet acquainted with its use as a dye.

Nos. 76 and 77.   Grislea Tomentosa.

Vernacular - $\begin{cases} (Beng.) & - & \text{Dhae-phul.} \\ (Hind.) & - & \text{Dhai.} \\ (Tel.) & - & \text{Godari.} \end{cases}$

This plant is found in every part of the continent of India. The flowers are used as a red dye, and with the bark of Calysaccion longifolium and indigo as a green dye on cloth.

No. 78.   Gushum Lai.

A substance from Kane Hill which gives a black dye.

No. 79.   Hedyotis Umbellata.

Vernacular - $\begin{cases} (Sing.) & - & \text{Choya.} \\ (Tam.) & - & \text{Saya.} \end{cases}$

This plant grows on the Coromandel coast, and is called in England " Chay " and " Indian Madder." The root gives a very good and durable red dye for cotton cloth, and a purple and brown orange dye are also procured from it.

No. 80.   Hirakus.

A substance used in dyeing in Hyderabad.

No. 81. HIRMICH.

An Indian dyestuff.

No. 83. GALL NUTS.

Vernacular - (*Hind.*) - Haldo.

Gall nuts are found in the Nizam's territory, where they are used for dyeing black on silks.

No. 84. HYMENODYCTION EXCELSUM.

Vernacular -$\begin{cases} (Hind.) & -\begin{cases} \text{Kala bachuak.} \\ \text{Bundarn.} \end{cases} \\ (Tel.) & - \text{Chetippa.} \end{cases}$

This tree is common all round the foot of the Neilgherrie and in the mountainous parts of the Circars. In England it is called Cedar wood. The bark is used for tanning leather.

No. 85. INDIGOFERA TINCTORIA.

Vernacular -$\begin{cases} (Guz., Hind.) & - \text{Nil.} \\ (Burm.) & - \text{Main-ay.} \\ (Malay) & - \text{Nila.} \end{cases}$

This plant is extensively grown in India, as well as in many other parts of the world. It yields the substance called indigo, which is well known to all connected with the dyeing of textile fabrics, as producing a good and permanent blue colour. Indigo is also much used along with yellow tinctorial substance in order to obtain many shades of green.

It is much to be lamented that its use for dyeing is restricted to wool and cotton. I am hoping to revive its application to silk dyeing, which since Macquer has gradually died out in Europe. It is the only durable blue on silk.

No. 87. IRON RUST.

Vernacular -$\begin{cases} (Burm.) & - \text{Than Khya.} \\ (Mal.) & - \text{Tai Basi.} \\ (Tam.) & - \text{Tuphu.} \end{cases}$

This substance, used by dyers in India, is produced in Shikarpur at a price of Rs. 8 per maund.

No. 88. JASMINUM GRANDIFLORA.

Vernacular -$\begin{cases} (Burm.) & - \text{Myat lac.} \\ (Hind.) & -\begin{cases} \text{Chambeli.} \\ \text{Jati.} \end{cases} \end{cases}$

A plant grown in India and used in Hyderabad with the seeds of Morinda citrifolia and other ingredients for dyeing red on Khadi cloth.

No. 89. JATROPHA GLANDULIFERA.

Vernacular -$\begin{cases} (Tam.) & - \text{Addale.} \\ (Tel.) & - \text{Nila amida.} \end{cases}$

This plant is a native of the East Indies, and grows in the Deccan and the Northern Circars. The leaves are used for dyeing green. One maund of them in a dried state will dye 1,280 yards of cloth an apple green colour.

No. 90. KAHU.

A dyestuff from the Berars yielding a brown colour.

No. 91. KAIS.

An Indian dyestuff, of which 50 maunds per annum come from Dadhur to Shikarpur, and are bought at Rs. 4 per maund.

No. 92 KAUNA BARK.

The bark of a tree growing in Ceylon. Used tinctorially in India.

Nos. 93 and 94. LAWSONIA INERMIS.

Vernacular $-\begin{cases} (Beng., Hind.) & - \text{ Mehndi.} \\ (Tel.) & - & - \text{ Iveni.} \end{cases}$

A shrub which grows all over India and many other Oriental countries. It is the Camphire of the Bible. A reddish brown substantive dye is procured from the leaves, which is used in the East for dyeing ordinary stuffs. The women of Turkey and other Oriental countries use it for dyeing the tips of their fingers, to which it imparts a beautiful rose colour. It is best known under the name " Henna." The Arabs use it to dye the manes and tails of their horses a reddish orange colour. It is also used among some men in the East to dye their beards.

No. 95. LIME.

Vernacular $-\begin{cases} (Hind.) & - \text{ Chuna.} \\ (Mal.) & - \text{ Tur.} \\ (Tam.) & - \text{ Chunambu.} \end{cases}$

This substance is used as a mordant in dyeing in Shikarpur, Jacobabad, and the Central Provinces.

No. 96. LORANTHUS LONGIFLORUS.

Vernacular $-\begin{cases} (in\ Kangra) & - \text{ Pand.} \\ (in\ the\ Punjab) - \text{ Banda.} \\ (Sutlej) & - & - \text{ Amut.} \end{cases}$

A tree which grows in the Punjab and on the Himalaya mountains. The bark is used by tanners.

No. 97. MAHOLI.

This substance, which yields a red dye, is found in all parts of Oudh forest. I do not know its scientific name.

Nos. 98 and 99. MALLOTUS PHILLIPENSIS.

Vernacular $-\begin{cases} (Sansc.) & - \text{ Kambha.} \\ (Mahr.) & - \text{ Sendri.} \end{cases}$

This plant is common all over British India.

The powder brushed off the ripe capsules and collected forms a most valuable dyeing material, although at present it has been very little employed in the tinctorial industry of Europe. It produces on silk mordanted with carbonate of soda and alum a most beautiful variety of shades of golden yellow and orange, and is so rich in colouring matter as to contain $70°/_0$ or $80°/_0$. It appears to be very permanent, for three samples I dyed with it (*see* No. 44 in the case of wild silks) do not seem to have lost any colour exposed to bright sun for the first two months of the Exhibition.

No. 100. MANGIFERA INDICA.

Vernacular -
{ (Malay) - Manga.
{ (Sansc.) - Amra.
{ (Hind.) - Am.

This tree is very extensively cultivated in India, and is known in England as the Mango tree. Gallic acid is said to be produced from the seed. but it is most probably tannic acid.

No. 101. MAO NUTGAO.

Probably synonymous with Mangifera Indica quod vide.

No. 102. MELIA AZEDARACH.

Vernacular -
{ (Hind.)   - - Drek.
{ (Hind. and Mahr.) - Nim.
{ (Tel.)   - - Vepa manu.

A plant common in Northern India and useful for tanning.

No. 103. MEMECYLON TINCTORIUM.

Vernacular -
{ (in Bombay) - Anjun.
{ (Mahr.) -   - Kurpa.
{ (Tam.) -   - Kasha maram.

This plant grows in the Malay peninsula, Tenasserim, and Coromandel. The leaves yield a yellow dye.

No. 104. MIMOSA ABSTERGENS.

Vernacular -
{ (Hind.) - Sikka-kai.
{ (Tel.) - Seekayah.

Grows in Mysore. The pods or legumes are used in India instead of soap for washing the head.

No. 105. MIMOSA SIRISSA.

Vernacular -
{ (Mahr.) {
  - Sirissa.
  - Chi.
  - Sal.

Used tinctorially in India.

No. 106. MORINDA ANGUSTIFOLIA.

A plant found on the Garro Hills, Assam, and used for dyeing scarlet.

Nos. 107 and 108.   MORINDA CITRIFOLIA.

Vernacular $\left\{\begin{array}{l}(Hind.) \\ (Burm.) \\ (Mahr.) \\ (Tel.)\end{array}\right.$ $\begin{array}{l}\text{-   Al.   Ach.   Ak.} \\ \text{-   Yai-yoe.} \\ \text{-   Bartondie.} \\ \text{-   Maddi chettu.}\end{array}$

A small tree common in Kotah and Boondee. It is much cultivated in the Bombay Presidency, and grows also in that of Madras, as well as in Pegu, Cochin China, and the Moluccas. From the roots and bark a scarlet colouring matter is procured which is used in India for dyeing handkerchiefs, turbans, &c. It is employed also to assist more expensive dyes in giving a red colour to yarn and cloth, the red thread used in carpet making being entirely dyed with it.

No. 109.   MORINDA EXSERTA.

Vernacular $\left\{\begin{array}{l}(Beng.) \\ (Burm.)\end{array}\right.$ $\begin{array}{l}\text{-   Bun-uch.} \\ \text{-} \left\{\begin{array}{l}\text{Mhan-bin.} \\ \text{Aya.}\end{array}\right.\end{array}$

A small tree of the Circars, Bengal, and Burmah, which like other Morindas yields a red dye.

No. 110.   MORINDA LANCEOLATA.

Vernacular $\left\{ (Hind.) \right.$ - $\left\{\begin{array}{l}\text{Moona.} \\ \text{Marum.}\end{array}\right.$

A plant of Bengal which yields a yellow dye.

No. 111.   MORINDA TINCTORIA.

Vernacular $\left\{\begin{array}{l}(Beng., Hind.) \\ (Tel.) \\ (Sans.)\end{array}\right.$ $\begin{array}{l}\text{-   Al.   Uch.   Ach.} \\ \text{-   -   Maddi-chettu.} \\ \text{-   -   Uchyuta.}\end{array}$

A small tree, supposed to be the same as M. Citrifolia in its wild state. It is pretty common in every part of India, and is largely cultivated at Ganjam, Gumsur, Boondee, Kotah, and other places. The bark of the root is used to dye red, the colour is fixed with alum, but it is neither bright nor durable. The roots may also be made to yield a beautiful golden yellow on cotton.

No. 112.   MORINDA UMBELLATA.

Vernacular $\left\{\begin{array}{l}(Burm.) \\ (Malay) \\ (Tam.)\end{array}\right.$ $\begin{array}{l}\text{-   Aya.} \\ \text{-   Mang kudu.} \\ \text{-   Nuna maram.}\end{array}$

A plant found in the western parts of India, Courtallam, and Malabar. The roots yield a yellow dye, and with the addition of Sapan wood a red dye for cotton.

No. 113.   MULTANIS.

An Indian dyestuff not used at present, as far as I am aware, in Europe.

No. 114. NEEPASAY GLAY.

The root of an Indian plant used as a dyeing material in Pegu.

No. 115. NEEPASAY GYER.

The root of a plant growing in Pegu and used in dyeing both red and yellow on silk and cotton.

No. 116. NYCTANTHES ARBORTRISTIS.

Vernacular - { (*Beng.*) - Shioli.
{ (*Mahr.*) - Pahar-butti.
{ (*Sans.*) - Sephalica.

This plant grows in Ajmeer. The tubes of the corollas yield a most beautiful though transient yellow on silk and cotton.

No. 117. ODINA WODIER.

Vernacular - { (*Burm.*) - Na-bhay.
{ (*Hind.*) - Kiamil.
{ (*Tam.*) - Ani-carra.

A tree growing on the Coromandel mountains, in Bengal, and Travancore. The gum which exudes from the trunk of the tree is used as a thickening for the colours in printing on cloth. The bark is used in Oudh for dyeing brown.

No. 118. ORYZA SATIVA.

Vernacular - { (*Ar.*) - Aruz.
{ (*Malay*) - Padi.

The rice plant, which grows all over India. The husk of rice is used tinctorially in India, but not yet, as far as I am aware, in Europe.

No. 119. PARMELIA CHAMCADULIS.

A lichen, gathered on the Himalaya and used in India in dyeing. Amongst the Himalaya it is known by the names of " Chalchalira " and " Ausneh."

No. 120. PAPDI.

Synonymous with carbonate of soda, quod vide.

Nos. 121 and 122. PHYLLANTHUS EMBLICA.

Synonymous with Emblica officinalis, quod vide.

No. 123. PINUS EXCELSA.

Vernacular - { (*in the Punjab*) - Biar.
{ (*Beas. Sutlej, &c.*) - Kail.

A tree growing in Narambethy, Nepal, Simla, Bootan, Sirmoor, and Gurhwal.

No. 124.   PINUS LONGIFOLIA.

Vernacular - (*Hind*) - { Chir. Sulla. Thausa.

A tree growing on the Himalaya, in the entrance to Nepal, in the Cheree Pass, and along the Tonse and Jumna rivers.

Nos. 125 and 126.   PISTACIA VERA.

Vernacular - (*Hind.*) - { Fistak. Pista.

This plant grows in many parts of Asia. The galls and flowers are used for dyeing a light red colour on silk.

No. 127.   POTASH.

Vernacular - { (*Hind.*) - Khar jowkshur. (*Tam.*) - Manu-uppu.

This substance is produced in Jacobabad, and is used for cleaning silk before dyeing.

No. 128.   PTEROCARPUS MARSUPIUM.

Vernacular - { (*Beng.*) - Y'egy, Vaygah. (*Hind.*) - Bibla, Pit shala. (*Mahr.*) - Bheulah.

A tree of southern India and Malabar. The wood contains a yellow colouring matter extensively used in India in dyeing and calico printing.

No. 129.   PUNICA GRANATUM.

Vernacular - { (*Hind.*) - Anaar-darim. (*Tam.*) - Madalum palam.

The Pomegranate tree, common in Bombay. The rind of the pomegranate is used for tanning and also produces a deep shade of yellow on cotton.

No. 130.   QUERCUS INCANA.

An Indian oak, the galls of which are used for tanning and for dyeing black.

Nos. 131 and 132.   QUERCUS INFECTORIA.

Vernacular - (*Hind.*) - Majoo-phal.

An oak tree growing in various parts of Asia. The galls and bark are used in tanning.

No. 133.   RASUM BUTI.

An Indian dyestuff not used, as far as I am aware at present, in Europe.

No. 134.   RHUS KAKRASINGHEE.

Vernacular - (*Hind.*) - { Kakur. Kakra.

A plant found in Kangra, the Himalaya, and Rumaon. Its pods are used for tanning.

No. 135. RUBIA MUNJISTA.

Vernacular - $\begin{cases} (Beng.) & - & \text{Aruna.} \\ (Hind.) & - & \text{Munjit.} \\ (Tam.) & - & \text{Sawil kodi.} \end{cases}$

A plant growing in Assam, Nepal, and Bombay. In England it is called "Indian madder," and the roots, stems, and large branches yield a red dye, which is, no doubt, much similar to that yielded by R. Tinctorium.

No. 136. RUBIA TINCTORIUM.

Vernacular - (Hind.) - Menjithe.

This plant is grown all over India and Ceylon. Its root yields the valuable dyeing material known as madder, which is so extensively used in Europe by both dyers and calico printers, and produces most beautiful and permanent shades of red and scarlet on cotton silk and wool.

No. 137. RUNG GACH.

An Indian dyestuff, not yet used, as far as I am aware, in Europe.

No. 138. SAKRA BERI.

An Indian dyestuff, not used at present, as far as I am aware, in Europe.

No. 139. SEMICARPUS ANACARDIUM.

Vernacular - $\begin{cases} (Beng.) & - & \text{Bhela.} \\ (Burm.) & - & \text{Chai-bin.} \\ (Hind.) & - & \text{Bhalawan.} \\ (Mahr.) & - & \text{Bibooa.} \end{cases}$

This plant is found in Madras and Bombay. The nuts are used in dyeing as a mordant, and a black juice is also extracted from them which is used to mark all kinds of cotton cloth.

No. 140. SESAMUM INDICUM.

Vernacular - $\begin{cases} (Burm.) & - & \text{Huan.} \\ (Beng., Hind.) & - & \text{Til.} \\ (Sansc.) & - & \text{Tila.} \end{cases}$

This plant is found all over India. Potash is obtained from it which (as stated under the head of "Potash") is used for cleaning silk previously to dyeing.

No. 141. SHINGRUF.

An Indian dyestuff, not known at present, as far as I am aware, in Europe.

No. 142. SOYMIDA FEBRIFUGU.

Vernacular - $\begin{cases} (Beng.) & - & \text{Rohuna.} \\ (Hind.) & - & \text{Rohitaka.} \\ (Tam.) & - & \text{Shem-maram.} \end{cases}$

This tree is found in Coimbatore, Cuddapah, and the mountainous districts of India. The bark dyes brown of various shades, according to the nature of the cloth.

No. 143. SAFFLOWER CAKE.

The flowers of Carthamus tinctoria, quod vide.

No. 144. SULPHUR.

Vernacular $\bullet$ $\begin{cases} (Burm.) & \text{-} & \text{Kan.} \\ (Malay.) & \text{-} & \text{Balirang.} \\ (Tam.) & \text{-} & \text{Gendagum.} \end{cases}$

This substance, much used for bleaching purposes, is found in India, in the regions of both active and extinct volcanoes. The price in Shikarpur, to where about 50 maunds annually come from Kachi, is Rs. 12 per maund.

Nos. 145 and 146. SYMPLOCOS RACEMOSA.

Vernacular $\bullet$ $\begin{cases} (Hind., Beng.) & \text{-} & \text{Lodh.} \\ (Mahr.) & \text{-} & \text{Hoora.} \\ (Tel.) & \text{-} & \text{Lodduga.} \end{cases}$

This tree grows in Nepaul, Kumaon, and Bengal. The bark of the root is sold in India at one rupee for four seers and is used for dyeing reds. On silk a beautiful shade of deep crimson may be produced by it.

No. 147. TAGETES ERECTA.

Vernacular - (*Hind.*) - Genda.

This plant, which grows in Oudh, yields a yellow dye which is transient.

Nos. 148 and 149. TAMARIX ORIENTALIS.

Vernacular - *in the Punjab* $\begin{cases} \text{-} & \text{Ghuz.} \\ \text{-} & \text{Farwa.} \end{cases}$

This tree grows on the Punjab plains and in Peshawur. The Galls, termed in Hindustani "Bari mai," are employed as a mordant in dyeing silk, and in parts of the Punjab the flowers also are used for dyeing. The bark is used in India for tanning.

No. 150. TERMINALIA ALATA.

Vernacular $\begin{cases} (Hind.) & \text{-} & \text{Urjan.} \\ (Mahr.) & \text{-} & \text{Kunjul.} \\ (Sansc.) & \text{-} & \text{Arjuna.} \end{cases}$

A tree growing in the Punjab and the Peninsula. The bark is used for tanning the skins of deer, goats, &c.

Nos. 151 and 152. TERMINALIA BELLERICA.

Vernacular $\begin{cases} (Beng.) & \text{-} & \text{Buhura.} \\ (Mahr.) & \text{-} & \text{Berda.} \\ (Sansc.) & \text{-} & \text{Bahira.} \end{cases}$

This plant grows in Ceylon, Pegu, and the Peninsula of India. The fruit is used for tanning leather, and a yellow dye is obtained from the galls.

Nos. 153, 157, 158, 159, 160.   TERMINALIA CHEBULA.

Vernacular
{
(*Beng.*) - Hari tuki.
(*Hind.*) - Har.
(*Mahr.*) - Heerda.
}

This tree grows in Ceylon, both Peninsulas of India, Nepaul, and the Punjab. The bark is used for tanning leather. The galls, too, are used for tanning as well as for making ink, and they produce a durable yellow colour on chintz and carpet yarns. The oval fruits, which are termed myrabolans, also contain much tannin, and with alum yield a good durable yellow dye, and with salts of iron a black dye is produced.

No. 154.   TERMINALIA CITRINA.

Vernacular
{
(*Beng.*) - Huri tuki.
(*Hind.*) - Harra.
(*Sansc.*) - Liba.
}

This plant is found in Assam, Khassya hills, and the Kotah jungles. It yields a yellow dye.

No. 155.   TERMINALIA CATAPPA.

Vernacular
{
(*Beng.*) - Badam.
(*Hind..*) - Badami.
(*Sansc.*) - Ingudi.
(*Tel.*) - Vadom.
}

A tree growing in the Molucccas, both Peninsulas of India, Deccan, Bengal, Madras, and Bombay.

The bark and leaves yield a black pigment, with which the natives dye their teeth and make Indian ink. Tussah silk worms feed on the leaves.

Nos. 161, 162, and 163.   TERMINALIA TOMENTOSA.

Vernacular
{
(*Beng.*) - Ashan. Usan.
(*Hind.*) - Asan.
(*Mahr.*) - Eyn.
}

A tree growing on the Malabar coast, the Concans, Monghir, Rajmahal, Oudh, the N.W. Provinces and Manbhoom. The bark is astringent and is used for dyeing black.

Nos. 164 and 165.   THESPESIA POPULNEA.

Vernacular
{
(*Beng.*) - Poresh.
(*Hind.*) - Parhari-pipal.
(*Mahr.*) - Bendi.
(*Tam.*) - Pursa maram.
}

A tree growing in Ceylon and Southern India, and known in England as the Tulip tree. The capsules are used by the Cingalese for dyeing yellow. The flower buds and unripe fruit also yield a yellow viscid juice, useful as a dye, and a thick deep red coloured oil is expressed from the seeds.

No. 166. VENTILAGO MADERASPATENA.

Vernacular - (*Tel.*) $\begin{cases} \text{Erra chiratah.} \\ \text{Surugudu.} \end{cases}$

This plant is common in Mysore, Ceylon, and the Indian Peninsula, and it is also found in Tenasserim. It is known in England as the Purple Chuckway. In Mysore an orange red dye is procured from it.

No. 167. WOODFORDIA FLORIBUNDA.

Vernacular - *Hind.* - Kangra.

A plant growing in the Punjab. Its use is not known at present, as far as I am aware, as a dyestuff in Europe.

No. 168. WRIGHTIA TINCTORIA.

Vernacular - $\begin{cases} (in\ Bombay.) & - & \text{Bhur-kuri.} \\ (Hind., Mahr.) & - & \text{Kala-koodoo.} \\ (Tam.) & - & \text{Pala maram.} \end{cases}$

The plant grows in Coimbatore, Godavery, and other forests of the Madras Presidency, and is very common in all the forests of Bombay. The leaves afford an inferior kind of indigo called "Pala-indigo."

No. 169. ZIZYPHUS JUJUBA.

Vernacular - $\begin{cases} (Ar.) & - & \text{Zruf.} \\ (Beng.) & - & \text{Kulyach.} \\ (Hind.) & - & \text{Nazak.} \end{cases}$

A tree growing throughout British India and Ceylon. It has in England the name of "Ber tree." In the north of India this tree bears a kind of lac called "Beree-ki-lakh," used for dyeing leather, cotton, and silk.

No. 170.

Mr. Locke's very interesting album of cloths and yarns dyed in colours produced by dyestuffs indigenous to Bengal.

No. 171. RED OCHRE.

Vernacular - $\begin{cases} \text{Tha kar.} \\ \text{Tholas saupar.} \end{cases}$

No. 172. TERMINALIA CHEBULA.

This plant is found in Manbhoom, and its fruit, which is termed "Myrabolans," yields a black dye, and is used for tanning.

No. 173. COCCUS LACCA.

Vernacular - Aragu.

A plant found in Mysore, and from which lac dye is obtained.

Nos. 174, 182, 183, 187. CARBONATE OF SODA.

Vernacular
$\begin{cases} \text{Dulla.} \\ \text{Dulla undata.} \\ \text{Bhushee.} \\ \text{Nemuk dulla.} \end{cases}$

This substance comes from Loonar Lake and the Berars, and is used in the manufacture of soap, and as a substitute for soap, also as a mordant in silk dyeing.

No. 175. CAESALPÍNIA SAPPAN.

Vernacular - Bakam.

This plant, the wood of which is used for dyeing red on silk, is found all over S.E. Asia.

No. 176. TERMINALIA BELLERICA.

Vernacular - Bahera.

A plant found in the N.W. Provinces, the fruits of which are used for tanning.

No. 177. PISTACIA TEREBINTHUS.

Vernacular - Boz gand.

The galls of this plant are used for tanning, and as a mordant for Kamila.

No. 178. TERMINALIA ANGUSTIFOLIA.

A plant found in the Peninsula. Its fruits are termed "Myrabolans," and like the other two species of myrabolans dye with alum a durable yellow, and with salts of iron black. They are also used for tanning.

No. 179. LACCA LACCIFERA.

A plant found in Mysore. Its galls, called Tamarix galls, are used for dyeing scarlet.

No. 180. PLUMBAGO ZEYLANICA.

Vernacular - Chitra-chita.

This plant comes from Mysore, and its root is used for dyeing black.

No. 181. SAPINDUS SP.

The pulp of the seeds of this plant is used for washing silk

No. 182. See No. 174.

No. 183. See No. 174.

No. 184. SAPINDUS SAPONARIA.

Vernacular - Aritha.

This plant is found in Bengal, and its berries, called "Soap berries," are used in dyeing as a detergent.

No. 185. BUTEA FRONDOSA.

Vernacular - Dhak.

This plant comes from the Berars, and its flowers are used for dyeing yellow.

No. 186. NYCTANTHES ARBORTRISTIS.

Vernacular - Shioli.

A plant found in Ajmeer, the flowers of which are used for dyeing a reddish yellow. .

No. 187. *See* No. 174.

No. 188. CEDRELA TOONA.

Vernacular - Toona. Tunna.

This tree is found in Bengal, and its bark is very astringent.

No. 189. COCCAS CACTI.

Vernacular - Kermij.

An insect found in Mysore, the dried bodies of which constitute cochineal, a substance extensively used for dyeing red and scarlet on silk and wool.

My authorities for the native uses of the foregoing dyestuffs are the Commissioners of the several districts in India, who were instructed by the India Office in 1874 to collect India dyestuffs and information concerning them, also Balfour's Cyclopædia of India, and the interesting and instructive Album containing dyed samples of cloths and yarns of silk, wool, and cotton beautifully arranged and described by H. II. Locke, Esq., Secretary of the Economic Museum, Calcutta, &c., to which I have great pleasure in calling attention, &c. (*See* No. 170.)

THOMAS WARDLE,
Leek, Staffordshire.

LONDON:
Printed by GEORGE EDWARD EYRE and WILLIAM SPOTTISWOODE,
Printers to the Queen's most Excellent Majesty.
For Her Majesty's Stationery Office.
[G 203.—500.—10/78.]

www.ingramcontent.com/pod-product-compliance
Lightning Source LLC
Chambersburg PA
CBHW021603270326
41931CB00009B/1352